Morning Coffee

Drawings by

GLEN G. GREENWALT

MORNING COFFEE. Copyright © 2012 by Glen Greenwalt. All rights reserved. Manufactured in China. No part of this book may be used or reproduced in any manner whatsoever without written permission except in the case of brief quotations embodied in critcal articles and reviews. For information address HarperCollins Publishers, 10 East 53rd Street, New York, NY 10022.

HarperCollins books may be purchased for educational, business, or sales promotional use. For information please write: Special Markets Department, HarperCollins Publishers. 10 East 53rd Street, New York, NY 10022.

Book design by Kathleen A. Servidio

ISBN: 9781883285524

12 13 14 15 16 SCP 10 9 8 7 6 5 4 3 2 1

A Coffee-Lover's Introduction

I always book hotels with a coffeemaker in the room. I bring my own, literally: my husband and I actually own a coffee farm in the Dominican Republic. How much more of a coffee control freak can you be? You love your good coffee so much, you can't trust anyone else, not just to make it, but to grow it!

But just because I am a coffee lover doesn't mean that I love anything having to do with coffee. I have high standards. I don't like that some splashy books are called coffee-table books. Only the best books deserve to be associated with the name of "coffee."

You are holding in your hands such a one. What a delight to get acquainted with so many likeminded souls, from Malcolm X to Ronald Reagan, from Unknown to T. S. Eliot, all of whom have had something to say about coffee: biting, sharp, hitting-the-spot, just like a good cup of coffee. And the pleasure of this book is not just in the mind, but in the eye. Glen G. Greenwalt's drawings draw you in, make you muse and amuse you.

You are in for a total treat: a coffee-table book as good as the best cup of coffee you have ever had!

—Julia Alvarez
Author of *A Cafecito Story* and *A Wedding in Haiti:*
The Story of a Friendship

Author's Note

The drawings in the three-book series — *Morning Coffee, Afternoon Tea*, and *Evening Wine* — grew out of my observations of people who come together to swap stories with friends, laugh, debate politics, interview for a job, read the paper or a book, or simply stare out of the window.

I have taught college religion and philosophy, but in my forties, at the encouragement of a colleague, I purchased a sketchbook. Drawing provided me a way of observing life with greater care than my own casual observations or academic studies had ever disclosed. At fifty-five, I finished a graduate degree in figurative studies.

I could draw a perfect likeness of a model holding a pose over several hours, but to learn how to draw people in motion, I began sketching in my local New York City coffee shop. Later, I moved out west, where I added several tea houses and a bistro to my favorite places to draw.

At first, I would hide the fact that I was drawing people. But they always noticed, and almost without exception, they were flattered, often adjusting their clothing or hair. If anyone appeared uncomfortable, or too posed, I would move on. I simply wanted to capture the everyday moments of life that usually go unobserved, to record how tea, coffee, and wine are the lubricants of social interaction, or of sweet solitude.

These books are a celebration of shared moments in our lives through my pen and ink — accompanied by the words of wiser people than I.

Glen Greenwalt, Seattle, 2012

I have measured out my life
with coffee spoons.

T. S. ELIOT

glen greenwalt
2007

Coffee smells like
freshly ground heaven.

JENI LANE ADAMS

glen greenwa
2007

A mathematician is
a machine for turning
coffee into theorems.

PAUL ERDÖS

glen greenwalt
2006

Do I like my coffee black?
There are other colors?

AUTHOR UNKNOWN

It is inhumane, in my opinion, to force
people who have a genuine medical need
for coffee to wait in line behind people
who apparently view it as some kind
of recreational activity...

DAVE BARRY

glen greenwalt
2017

I don't have a problem with caffeine.
I have a problem without caffeine.

AUTHOR UNKNOWN

glen greenwalt
2007

I orchestrate my morning
to the tune of coffee.

HAM MAHTAN

The morning cup of coffee has an exhilaration about it which the cheering influence of the afternoon or evening cup of tea cannot be expected to reproduce.

OLIVER WENDALL HOLMES SR.

Wake up and smell the coffee.

ANN LANDERS

glen greenwelt
2008

No coffee can be good in the mouth that does not first send a sweet offering of odor to the nostrils.

HENRY WARD BEECHER

glengreenwa
2010

They shift coffee-houses and chocolate-houses from hour to hour, to get over the insupportable labor of doing nothing.

RICHARD STEELE

glen green wall
2007

The coffee was so strong it snarled
as it lurched out of the pot.

BETTY MAC DONALD

glen greenwalt
2007

Sleep is a symptom
of caffeine deprivation.

AUTHOR UNKNOWN

glen greenwalt
2007

Coffee is the best thing to
douse the sunrise with.

DREW SIRTORS

glen greenwalt
200—

Retirement is one great coffee break.

AUTHOR UNKNOWN

glen greenwalt
2007

The powers of a man's mind are
directly proportioned to the quantity
of coffee he drinks.

Sir James Mackintosh

glen greenwalt
2007

Coffee is the common man's gold,
And like gold,
It brings to every person the feeling
Of luxury and nobility.

SHEIK ABD-AL-KADIR

glen greenwalt
2009

Coffee, which makes the politician wise,
And see through all things with his
half-shut eyes.

ALEXANDER POPE

glen greenwalt
2007

That Grave and Wholesome Liquor,
that heals the Stomach, makes the Genius
quicken, Relieves the Memory, rewires
the Sad, and cheers the Spirits,
without making Mad.

Anonymous Poem

glen greenwalt
2006

Tobacco, coffee, alcohol, hashish,
prussic acid, strychnine are weak dilutions:
the strongest poison is time.

RALPH WALDO EMERSON

Conscience keeps more people
awake than coffee.

AUTHOR UNKNOWN

glen greenwood
2007

My blood type is Fulgers:
House Blend

AUTHOR UNKNOWN

glen greenwalt
2007

Coffee should be black as Hell,
strong as death, and sweet as love.

TURKISH PROVERB

glen greenwalt
2008

I would rather suffer with
coffee than be senseless.

NAPOLEON BONAPARTE

glen greenwalt
2007

Good coffee is like friendship:
rich and warm and strong.

PAN AMERICAN COFFEE BREWERS

Coffee makes us severe,
And grave,
And philosophical.

Jonathan Swift

glen greenwalt
2006

The discovery of coffee has enlarged
the realm of illusion and given
more promise to hope.

ISIDORE BOURDON

glen greenwalt
2007

I'd stop drinking coffee,
but I am no quitter.

AUTHOR UNKNOWN

glen greenwalt
2007

I know a song of Africa—I thought—of the
Giraffe, and the African, the moon lying
on her back, of the plows in the fields,
and the sweaty face of coffee-pickers,
does Africa know a song of me?

ISAK DINESEN

glen greenwalt
2007

Look here steward, if this is coffee,
I want tea; but if this is tea,
then I want coffee.

PUNCH

glen greenwalt
2007

Like a small gray
Coffee pot
Sits the squirrel.

HUMBERT WOLFE

glengreenwatt
2007

It is just like when you've got some coffee that's too black, which means it's too strong. What do you do? You integrate it with cream, you make it weak. But if you pour too much cream in it, you won't ever know you ever had coffee. It use to be hot, it becomes cool. It use to be strong, it becomes weak. It use to wake you up, now it puts you to sleep.

MALCOLM X

glen greenwalt
2007

No one can understand the truth until
one drinks of coffee's frothy goodness.

SHEIK AD-AL-KADIR

glen greenwalt
2007

So great a University, I think there
ne'er was any; in which you may a
Scholar be, for a Penny.

DITTY FROM THE 1650'S REGARDING COFFEE-HOUSES

glen greenwatt
2008

Recipe for Coffee:
Black as the devil, hot as hell,
Pure as an angel,
Sweet as love.

TALLEYRAND

Glen Greenwalt
2007

Nancy Astor: If I were your wife I would put poison in your coffee!

Winston Churchill: If I were your husband I would drink it.

Consuelo Vanderbilt Balsan

glen greenwalt
2007

Thence to the Coffee-house, whither comes
Sir W. Petty and Captain Grant, and we fell in
talke… of musique; the universal character;
art of memory… and other most excellent
discourses to my great content, having not
been in so good company a while…

SAMUEL PEPYS

glen greenwall
2007

Good communication is just as
stimulating as black coffee, and just
as hard to sleep after.

ANNE MORROW LINDBERGH

glen greenwalt
2007

Never drink black coffee at Lunch; it will keep you awake in the afternoon.

RONALD REAGAN

Decaf? No, it's dangerous
to dilute my caffeine stream.

AUTHOR UNKNOWN

glen greenwalt
2007

Deja Brew: The feeling that you've
had this coffee before.

AUTHOR UNKNOWN

Everyone should believe in something.
I believe I'll have another cup of coffee.

AUTHOR UNKNOWN

glen greenwalt
2007

I am not yet convinced that any Access to men in Power gives a man more Truth or Light than the Politicks of a Coffee House.

JONATHAN SWIFT

glen greenwatt
2007

[Coffee is a] vile and worthless foreign novelty…
The fruit of a tree discovered by goats and
camels [which] burns up the blood, induces
palsies, impotence and leanness…

DOCTORS OF MARSEILLES

Coffee

Classics   Fall Favorite

Pumpkin Spice
is Back

glen greenwalt
2007

Coffee, the sober drink, the mighty nourishment of the brain, which unlike other spirits, heightens purity and lucidity; coffee, which clears the clouds of the imagination and their gloomy weight; which illuminates the reality of things suddenly with the flush of truth.

JULES MICHELET

glen greenwalt
2008

Why doth solid and serious learning decline,
and few or none follow it now in the university?
Answer: Because of coffee-houses where
they spend all their time.

ANTHONY WOOD

glen greenwalt
2008

Mothers are those wonderful people
who can get up in the morning before
the smell of coffee.

AUTHOR UNKNOWN

glen greenwalt
2007

Actually, this seems to be the basic need
of the human heart in nearly every
great crisis—a good cup of coffee.

ALEXANDER KING

BOOKS GAME M A

glen greenwalt
2007

As soon as you sit down to a cup of hot coffee,
your boss will ask you to do something which
will last until the coffee is cold.

AUTHOR UNKNOWN

glen greenwalt
2007

He was my cream, and I was
his coffee—And you poured us
together, it was something.

JOSEPHINE BAKER

glen greenwall
200

Chocolate, men, coffee—
some things are better rich.

AUTHOR UNKNOWN

glen greenwalt
2007

I like my coffee like women:
hot, strong, steamy.

AUTHOR UNKNOWN

glen greenwalt
2008

Acknowledgements

I would like to thank my teachers at the New York Academy of Art who taught me the rules of proportions and the construction of a beautiful form. Martha Mason, who through her own drawings taught me the beauty and energy of scribbling. Karen Fields, who watching me draw in a coffee shop, first suggested that my sketches should be published alongside quotations about coffee.

Helen Zimmermann, my agent, who believed in my project and transformed the idea I had for a regional book on Saturday mornings in my local coffee shop into three books, Morning Coffee, Afternoon Tea, and Evening Wine. Without her perseverance, as well as that of Carl Lennertz, this project would never have found a home with the wonderful people at Delphinium Books who made this dream come true. Thank you to Kathleen Servidio at HarperCollins for a beautiful book design.

Finally, I would like to thank the people who encouraged me throughout this project: my parents, Don and Rose Greenwalt; my sister Linda Tonsberg; my children, Natascha and Gavin, who are each successful artists in their own right; Dan Lamberton and Ron Jolliffe, who listened to hours of my worries; and Elena Mezisko, who not only encouraged me in this project, but added sparkle to my life.

About the Author

GLEN G. GREENWALT holds a PhD from Vanderbilt University and graduated Cum Laude from the New York Academy of Art. He has been teaching for over 20 years, currently as Adjunct Professor of Humanities at Shasta College in California.

The drawings in the three books grew out of studied observations of people who come together for social contact at coffee houses, tea rooms, and bistros. His quest was to explore and share this core experience of life through his drawings and the quotes he selected.